M000237717

The Garden of Eva

The collected works

of

Eva B. Carson

ANTHOLIC

PUBLISHING BY CBA

Copyright © 2019 Antholic

An imprint of
CBA Publishing Services, LLC
https://cbapub.com

Editing and layout by Christine Brown
Cover design and photo editing by Anna Talyn
Additional material by John E. Carson

Cover oil painting by Malanya Monette
https://creativedesigncircle.com

All rights reserved. No part of this book may be reproduced in any form or by any electronic means including storage and retrieval systems—except in the case of brief quotation embodied in critical articles and reviews—without express written consent from its publisher, except provided by the United States of America copyright law.

Photos used with permission.

First Edition 2019

ISBN-13: 978-1-7324746-7-3

Dedication

This book is dedicated to Eva B. Carson

and

All the flowers that grew from her garden.

The rain to the wind said,

"You push and I'll pelt."

They so smote the garden bed

That the flowers actually knelt,

And lay lodged—though not dead.

I know how the flowers felt.

— Robert Frost

Table of Contents

Foreword

Dark brown is the river,
Golden is the sand,
It flows along for ever,
With trees on either hand.

The opening lines of Robert Louis Stevenson's poem, *Where Go the Boats,* are indelibly etched into my memory and no doubt inspired my mother to write as she quoted them so often to me as a child in the 1950's.

Born in 1917, Eva B. Carson grew up in the days of the Great Depression, gangsters and *speakeasys.* The youngest of four girls from a poor family, whose father was forced to look for work in another state, life was often hard and things a young girl should not be exposed to were all too common. The poetry still being taught in the schools offered a respite from the life outside on the street.

In those years, people often did whatever was necessary to survive both physically and emotionally and the impressions made on young people often become, or bring out, their core beliefs and feelings.

The hard life pursued both my parents as they struggled financially to raise their children in an era of hard working and hard living people was not seen on television shows like *Leave it to Beaver.*

The wonderful world of the Fabulous Fifties was not to be had by everyone, especially the parents of ten children who relied solely on manual labor to keep a roof over their heads.

The loss of three children, twin girls and a boy, added to the emotional strain of my mother and father, as one drink after work often led to one too many and Mother dealt with her pain at home often the same way. Yet, Eva held on to the simple beauty of poems and the therapeutic effects of writing as a way to deal with the emotional river of trauma that ran through her life, often creating simple, yet thoughtful poems and just as often crafting mirrors of her soul.

Surrounded by children, she felt alone and often trapped as the width of the river between my parents grew too far to ford and they separated, floating one stop away from divorce where they floundered for the rest of their married life, reaching for but never grasping each other's hand as they had in the happy days of setting out together.

Through all the rapids she encountered, all the eddies that swirled, Eva chronicled the emotional journey of life in the poems contained in this book.

Though I encouraged her often to seek publication, she never did so, content with her one award from the World of Poetry.

It is our hope now that her words and her journey along that dark brown river will bring hope to others seeking the golden sand.

John Evan Carson

About This Book

Originally compiled and typeset long before the advent of the personal computer by her son, Mark Steven Carson, this volume consists of the known works of Eva B. Carson.

This book is the result of the dedicated effort of Christine Brown and Anna Talyn Carson; the author's grandchildren and owners of CBA Publishing Services, LLC.

The purpose of this book is to share the writing of Eva that might be unknown to family and friends and celebrate the life of the woman who brought so much into the world. Our hope is that it will bring joy to those who loved her, those who didn't get the chance to, and strangers in the wide world who might wish they had known this remarkable lady.

Poems

Eva as a young girl

Lady in Waiting

Lady in waiting—the heart of a girl
Off at last to see the world
The velvet and lace you never wore
Has found the time it waited for.

A tomboy in youth—no fancy dresses
A Cinderella with long blonde tresses
Making your way through trials and defeats
Living alone out on the streets.

The heart of a lady kept beating inside
As well as yourself for others you cried.

Late to the ball—your prince not in sight
You held on to your dream with all of your might.

The love you sought to match your own
To turn your house into a home
Was not to be found as your children grew
Though they tried to fill the void in you.

Lady in waiting—the heart of a girl
Big enough to love the whole wide world
Willing to give it all to one man
If he would reach out and take your hand…

But a lifetime of sorrow could not erase
The smile of a child that shown on your face.

A bat and a ball and a cap on your head…

Dreams of the world as you lay on your bed.

Lady in Waiting—the work is all done
Time to travel and walk in the sun
There you stand in your gown and lace
The hat on your head framing your face.

A lady awaiting her coach to arrive
Young and fair and so much alive!

Off to see the cosmos at will
With eyes to see beyond the next hill…

Though a Lady you are I still hear your call
A tomboy in Heaven with a bat and ball.

—John Evan Carson—1998

A Dream

I had a dream of the world one nite.

It turned slowly in a greenish-blue lite.

But where I was, I did not know.

For my body didn't show.

Yet, I looked down on this wonderous site.

I had a dream of the world one nite.

~Eva B. Carson~

A Little Beauty

I just wanted a little beauty in my life—that's all.

I just wanted someone to help me through

The strife that has been over me like a pall.

It would have been more humane to use the knife.

God!

I've done everything, but crawl.

Yet—I'm still full of life!

~Eva B. Carson~

A Way With Words

To have a way with words

That comfort and inspire.

To have a way with words

To give someone a desire

To rise ever and ever higher.

Words are meant to express thought.

Let mine be thoughtfully wrought.

~Eva B. Carson~

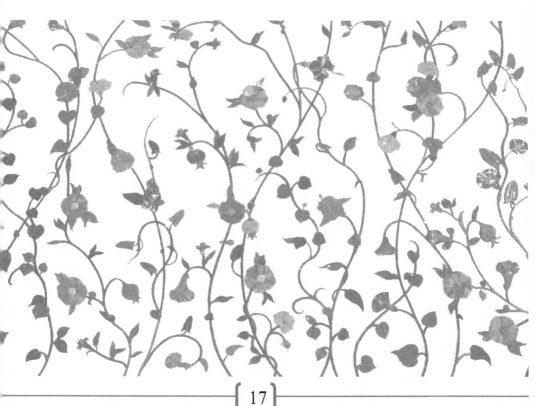

A Need

If there were a Garden of Eden,

You, I would have there.

To put a true meaning into a life without care.

For what is a garden

Without my dear one

To see all the beauty

That is under the sun?

~Eva B. Carson~

A Welcome Home

A soft breeze trembled

The gay blossoms and leaves.

The trees quivered impatiently…

It seemed to be as if they wanted

To bow to greet me.

For I was home.

~Eva B. Carson~

An Entertainer

I always wanted to be an entertainer.

But, never a clown!

I like to cheer people

Whether they're up or down.

I see sadness in a clown.

What do they hide behind their paint:

A sinner or a saint?

They have an element of sadness

That takes away gladness

Be it ever so faint!

~Eva B. Carson~

Cats

I love cats,

But I've never written a poem about these very

Lovely creatures that take over heart and home.

They eat all they can,

If it suits their taste.

If not—you can throw it in the waste!

Affectionate, independents,

Playful and great actors.

But, what makes a cat?

Why, these very same factors!

~Eva B. Carson~

Christmas

I love Christmas and all it means

There's nothing finer, so it seems.

But, once a year is not enough.

Every day, someone's stocking

You should stuff.

Put in all you have to give.

To all you care about.

It sounds impossible, I know!

But Santa does it in one nite!

And, through all that snow!

~Eva B. Carson~

Curly Cat

Curly cat,

Digger dog,

Squealy pig,

Fatso hog.

~Eva B. Carson~

Dogging Me

I have withstood lots of things.

Turmoil and strife…

But not the soul-twisting loneliness

That has dogged me all my life.

~Eva B. Carson~

Forever and a Day

When the day is dark and dreary,

And it's extra hard to be merry,

(For merry we must be)

To get through this life gracefully.

But, if it cannot be,

Have a glass of wine with me,

And look forward to eternity.

~Eva B. Carson~

Give and Take

Love should be elastic,

For it's "give and take."

Without love,

Something will break.

Be it you,

Or be it I,

This propulsion will fizzle

And die.

A shame!

For we all

Aim for the sky.

~Eva B. Carson~

Halloween

Tonite the moon is bright and clear

Tonite the little witches and goblins are here.

They form a band and roam the land,

And use naught but their open hand,

To get the grownups to go along

With their plan.

~Eva B. Carson~

Here Comes Santa Claus!

Here comes Santa Claus!

And he went right by!

So many kids are going to

Wonder why!

~Eva B. Carson~

Idealist

I want to be a vegetarian,

But I was raised to eat meat.

I try to cure myself by picturing

The animals on their feet.

Yes, I am an "Idealist"

(As far as the word goes);

In having the right to

My "yes's" and my "no's."

~Eva B. Carson~

It's an Emotion

Some fools think that love

Means "condescending."

On the contrary…

It raises one to

The greatest of height.

For "love" is not

Only a word,

It's an emotion that

Carries great might!

~Eva B. Carson~

It's Home

A house is not just a place

To hang your hat.

Oh, no—it is more than that.

It's a place where you can

Cook and clean,

Take a bath

And all that.

It's a place that's yours alone.

It's not heaven,

But it's home.

~Eva B. Carson~

John's M.D. Dance

I'll never forget

John's M.D. dance.

Boy! How Dad

And I did prance.

I never did ask him

If he had a much fun as I,

Dancing for his son.

I think he did, you see

As it was for John and M.D.!

(It sure helped me!)

~Eva B. Carson~

Let's Have

Let's have "Ye Merrie Olde Christmas."

One from the past.

One more Merrie Old Christmas.

One that will last.

~Eva B. Carson~

Life

Life is what you love.

Love is what you give.

Earth is where it's done.

End is sure to come.

~Eva B. Carson~

Loneliness

I saw a ghost

Upon the wall.

It loomed, wide and tall.

It spoke no word…

It gave no sign…

It did in fact,

Have no mind.

But mine.

I could give it body.

I could give it power.

I did neither…

Because of the hour.

~Eva B. Carson~

Moments

There were not many moments.

But there were some.

These are the moments from

Whence this poem comes.

I could make you laugh,

And feel at ease.

In fact, we giggled,

And I did it to please.

Those moments were so rare.

But I remember,

They were there.

~Eva B. Carson~

My Sitting Room

I get the late afternoon sun in my dining room.

But—I get the afterglow in my sitting room;

And I follow.

Sometimes, I like the gloom

That pervades my sitting room.

Then, I will not sit in my dining room;

When the sun is in full bloom.

~Eva B. Carson~

Old Floor Sweeper Me

Here's my broom,

But I'm not going to sweep the floor!

I'm going to sit on it,

And fly out the door!

I'll sail around at my ease,

I'll go here and there as I please.

I'll look for you,

And something more.

I want to feel the refreshing wind in my hair.

And hear all that

It whispers in my ear.

Let someone else take

Over the chore of sweeping

The dirt from the floor.

~Eva B. Carson~

Prayer

Please come over here and take my hand.

Look in my eyes and understand

That what you see is a need that's great.

Dear God—don't let it come too late.

How many times have I prayed this way?

Long ago,

Yesterday

And today.

~Eva B. Carson~

Shine, Shine

Shine, shine moon while you can.

For you'll soon be conquered by man.

You have a beauty and mystery

Out there in space.

But you'll never be the same

With man on your face.

~Eva B. Carson~

So Glad

Rock-A-Bye,

Kitty-Kat,

In that

Chair there.

I am so glad

That you are here.

~Eva B. Carson~

Something

A dog is something that curls.

A mole is something that burrows.

But a toe is something that taps.

~Eva B. Carson~

Stray

What do you do with a dog that's a stray?

Who has the heart to send him away?

Who left it alone on the street one day?

To follow the kids who can't stop the play.

I suppose that they feel

Someone will care.

Or, they couldn't have

Left it all alone there.

~Eva B. Carson~

The Elf in the Woods

Out in the woods and under a tree,

I saw a wee Elf—but he didn't see me!

He was sitting on a toadstool and humming away.

And, oh! His suit was cunning and gay!

I stood so still as I watched him there.

(Not even the wind ruffled my hair!)

His suit was so bright as the sun in the sky,

And brighter than bright was the blue of his eye.

A brown pointed cap sat straight on his head,

And the feather in it was marvelously red!

He seemed to be waiting for someone to come.

(I could tell by the way he continued to hum.)

I wanted to move, but did not dare,

For if I did—he'd know I was there!

Now Elves are good, and they are kind,

But to be seen—they mind!

He grew tired of humming, as I of my pose.

As he scratched his head, I wiggled my nose.

For a sneeze was coming that couldn't be stopped.

And as I sneezed, down from the toadstool he hopped!

He went 'round the tree, then stuck out his head;

Waved the brown cap with the feather of red.

Then he was gone, I don't know where.

But, when I go back—I hope he'll be there.

Now, I was lucky to see this sight;

As it was in the broad daylight!

Maybe some night when the moon is high,

We'll go looking for Elves, you and I.

~Eva B. Carson~

Editor's note: This poem was written for her youngest son, Ted, at the age of 11.

The Ostrich

The ostrich isn't so bad off

For sticking his head in the sand, I say.

I suggest that most people would be

Better off shutting their mouths

This very same way.

~Eva B. Carson~

To Be Loved Again

I'm through with crossword puzzles.

I'm through with solitaire.

I'm through being lonely

'Cause you don't care.

I'll toss away the books.

I'll toss away the cards.

I'll toss my head and change my looks.

It shouldn't be hard.

I'll remember my P's and Q's;

And count to ten,

'Cause I want to be in love

And be loved again.

~Eva B. Carson~

To My Cat

A kitty came to my house one day.

I said, "You're ugly, you'll have to go away."

But, he reached out a paw and put it to my face.

Such a gentle touch, and now he runs the place!

He's grown to be a beauty

And is loving and sweet.

And, I'll have him with me long;

If he stays away from the street.

~Eva B. Carson~

Twilight Rain in the City

It rained in the city.

(My hometown)

And each drop than came down

Bounced and leaped like a clown.

For the evening lights that came on

At the darkening of the day,

Made them gayer than gay.

Yes, this is the most flattering of lights.

For raindrops that come in the twilight.

~Eva B. Carson~

Yesteryear Again

They say it is wrong to dwell in the past.

(The days of yesteryear)

But, oh! How I wish I were there.

The winters were filled with white delight.

Warmth meant warmth then

And summers s-t-r-e-t-c-h-e-d

Out away beyond the bend.

And each night was just an end,

So you could have tomorrow—

Again and again and again.

~Eva B. Carson~

Do Not Stand at my Grave and Weep

Do not stand at my grave and weep,
I am not there, I do not sleep.
I am in the thousand winds that blow,
I am in the softly falling snow.
I am the gentle showers of rain,
I am the fields of ripening grain.
I am in the morning hush,
I am in the graceful rush
Of beautiful birds in circling flight,
I am the star shine of the night.
I am in the flowers that bloom,
I am in a quiet room.
I am the birds that sing,
I am in each lovely thing.
Do not stand at my grave and cry,
I am not there. I do not die.

—Mary Frye

The Link

Time has not touched
This place in my heart
There's a link between us
The world can't part.

No matter the times
We went our own way
No matter the times
When we had nothing to say…

We each have to be
Our own person—it's true
We each have to go
And do what we do.

With love and respect
Accepting each other
Alike but different
The same father and mother.

And when I crossover
To life without end
I'll watch for my brother—
And wait for my friend.

—John Evan Carson—1998

Photos

Eva as a young woman

Sisters: Myrtle, Elaine, Eva, Abby Sandberg

Eva and Howard Carson

Juliet, Gail, and Diane (daughters)

Sons Ted (also below), Mark, John

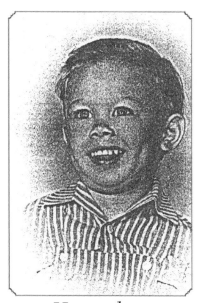

Howard

John

Mark

Ted

Afterword

As muddy as the river of Eva's life may have been, it nurtured both her garden of children and her garden of words.

Though I never heard her quote the whole poem, I am sure she knew and understood it and I now present it in closing this book. I know the readers of this volume of work, who have come to know the poet that Eva was, will see the flowering of the garden that she planted.

Where Go the Boats

Dark brown is the river,
Golden is the sand.
It flows along for ever,
With trees on either hand.

Green leaves a-floating,
Castles on the foam,
Boats of mine a-boating-
Where will all come home?

On goes the river
And out past the mill,
Away down the valley,
Away down the hill.

Away down the river,
A hundred miles or more
Other little children
Shall bring my boats ashore.

—Robert Louis Stevenson

Acknowledgements

The publisher would like to thank the many people who have made this collection possible.

Mark Carson, for compiling Eva's poems and pictures many years ago and preserving them for us all.

John Carson for his invaluable writing skills and insight in the additional material throughout the book.

Christine Brown and Anna Talyn for putting the book together, cover to cover.

Malanya Monette of Creative Design Circle for the oil painting of Eva featured on the cover.

Diane and Jim Shea for providing some of the pictures used in the book.

Marlene Carson, Howard Carson, Ted and Mary Carson, Gail Ripley and Juliet Anderson for their support of CBA.

And all of the many, many grandchildren, great grandchildren and beyond, as well as many other extended family. You are all a part of The Garden of Eva that has spread and blossomed and without her would not be here.

I hope you all enjoyed this walk in the garden with Eva!

About the Authors

Eva B. Carson (1917–1993)—One of four girls, who could have gone to Hollywood with her looks alone, Eva's life was tumultuous. Her giving heart was often tested and she walked the line between her ideals and the realities of life as she struggled to raise her family. Born Evabelle Sandberg, she changed her name to reflect her greatest desire, "Just let me be Eva."

John E. Carson—The author of several published novels and many published poems and works on display, John credits his mother with his love of writing and being understood. He has won several writing competitions, earned several 5 Star book reviews and has been continually published in the Old Huntsville Magazine for the past three years.

John teaches Creative Writing at the Huntsville Senior Center, in Huntsville, Alabama where he retired and lives with his wife and co-author, Marlene Rose Carson and his faithful sidekick, a rescue dog named Mr. Freckles.

Made in the USA
Lexington, KY
06 December 2019

58243753R00041